Patchwork Poems

90 years . . . 90 poems

Richard Allen Anderson

Vabella Publishing
P.O. Box 1052
Carrollton, Georgia 30112
www.vabella.com

©Copyright 2023 Richard Allen Anderson

All rights reserved. No part of the book may be reproduced or utilized in any form or by any means without permission in writing from the author. All requests should be addressed to the publisher.

Manufactured in the United States of America

13-digit ISBN 978-1-957479-63-7

10 9 8 7 6 5 4 3 2 1

Other books by Richard Allen Anderson
www.amazon.com/author/richardallenanderson

Poetry Collections:

Winter Weeds
Vabellla Publishing, 2019

Potholes in Memory Lane
Vabella Publishing, 2016

Another Season Spent
Vabella Publishing, 2013

Short Fiction Collection:

Taradiddle and Cookie Crumbs
tales of Love, Mystery and Adventure
Vabella Publishing, 2019

Illustrated for Children:

The Adventures of Diggerydoo and Taller Too
Vabella Publishing, 2016

Memoir

for the Good Times
Vabella Publishing, 2021

Family History

Family Album
Vabella Publishing 2022

Dedicated to my family
        past and present
                near and far

Patchwork Poems?

Google offers these possibilities when queried with the term "Patchwork."

"Pieced work" comprising discarded unused remnants carefully measured and cut to be easily pieced together.

"Sewing together pieces of fabric into a larger design"— suggesting the whole may be greater than the sum of its parts.

This is possibly an apt analogy to the human persona and character, akin to the notion, alluded to by Whitman when he notes, "I am large. I contain multitudes," that each of us is a composite being, and each of us comprises all of us, human commonality.

Webster confirms these choices and enlarges on the concept with multiple definitions and synonyms (50 in all).
Definition:
composed of miscellaneous or incongruous parts.
Select few synonyms:
Cento—a literary work made up of parts from other works
Collage—a creative work with various elements
Farrago—a confused mixture
Gallimaufry—variety of opinions
Pastiche—literary, musical or artistic collection
Potpourri—live or dead flower arrangements
Mélange—incongruous assortment
Menagerie—zoo like group
And my personal favorites incorporating the concept of delicious nourishment: gumbo, hash, jambalaya, stew, olio, smorgasbord and salmagundi.

These poems were written during a time when moments of personal joy were fewer, moments of disappointment and despair more frequent. The span of years included the final moments of the life of the woman I had spent 70 years admiring, loving, hating, attempting to understand and caring for when she bravely faced and endured increasingly cruel challenges to her physical and mental wellbeing.

Then she died and some of me died with her.

Writing became refuge and relief.

It was time also when the world population was attacked by a viral threat that has killed more than seven million and infected 100 times more, disrupting commerce, education, and all aspects of everyday life. Medical science to the rescue, holding ignorance, misinformation and the virus momentarily at bay.

During these years, the American nation became severely divided by extreme political ideologies to the degree personal relationships with family and friends were threatened, strained and even severed.

And Nature and civilizations are increasingly threatened by effects of the ever warming planet.

Yet impersonal time moves on. Appreciation for the miracles of life may emerge from observing the whole of nature's miracles and remembrance of better times.

These are the scraps and pieces alluded to in these patchwork poems, written in a variety of styles, sharing my personal thoughts and emotions, hopefully offering bits of philosophy, understanding and perhaps a few good laughs.

Richard Allen Anderson
August 2023

CONTENTS

Patchwork Poems?   ix

<u>Patch 1</u>
Patchwork Poems   3
My Muse Refuses   4
A Poem is Like a Pomme de Terre   5
Not A-mused   7
Per Apps   8
Progress   10
Ekphrasis on Poetry on a Page   12
Nevermore   13
Ghost Writers   14
Tattered Pages   15

<u>Patch 2</u>
Big Tip   19
Golden Years   20
Playing Games   21
New Years Eve   23
Love and Learn   24
Kintsukuroi   25
Changing Dimensions   27
One Day   29
Seasoned   30
The Thought   31
Cave Man   33
The Final Mystery   34
Ode and haiku to Covid-19   35
Miasma on America   36
We Need a Change of Climate   37
Apocalypse Revised   38
better ember than ash   39

CONTENTS (cont)

Patch 3

spring green leaves	43
yellow bird & tiny goldfinch	44
after the rain & disgruntled robin	45
camera captures & tiny warrior	46
spring breezes & dog days	47
autumn leaves & winter blankets	48
fly on my plate	49
fly on the wall	50
pesky devil fly	51
black ant	52
snowflake	53
humble dandelion	54
tenacious leaf & pewter skies	55
morning mist & puffed up cardinal	56
frost crystals & rays of dawn	57
full moon rising	58
moonlit shadows	59

Patch 4

Charlotte the Harlot	63
Spring Ahead	64
Thanks for Nothing Robert Pinsky	65
Parting Impressions	67
Heavenly Advice	68
He Who Hesitates	69
A Matter of Some Gravity	70
To Err	72
Despair the Hare	73
Dating Protocol	74
Whatever Happened to Eclectic	75
Autumnal	76
Unspoiled	77

CONTENTS (cont)

Patch 5
The Road We Took	81
Ice Cream and Cookies	82
in the deep of night	83
Tremors	84
Pas de deux	85
One Day at a Time	87
The Garden	89
What I Mean	90
Sometimes	93

Patch 6
Auto Biography	97
Optimist	98
Change of Pace	100
The Meaning of Life	101
I Am	102
Parental Guidance	103
Late Awakening	104
Q & A	105
Once	106
Saved	107
Sanctum	108
Vulnerable	110
My Way	111
Again	113
Decrepit	114

The Long and the Short of It	117
Acknowledgements	118

"Poetry is somebody standing up, so to speak, and saying, with as little concealment as possible, what it is for him or her to be on earth at this moment."

Galway Kinnell, Pulitzer Prize winning poet

Patchwork Poems

discarded, well-worn bits
patiently or impatiently accumulated over time
by a mind too frugal or too fearful to discard
puzzle pieces of uncertain utility
carefully measured, cut and reassembled

a patchwork of unrelated scraps
incongruent shapes, patterns, colors
now a whole thing again
offering comfort—even pleasure
out of stitched together joys, sorrows, dreams

My Muse Refuses

I'm waiting for ambition
To strike me once again,
Descending like the Holy Spirit
Visits some,

Like a pigeon from above,
Or should I say a dove,
To banish all this laziness that of late
Has dulled my spirit and my will.

But I don't know a remedy—
No magic potion or potent pill
To sweep away this malady,
For inspiration to return

To make my passions burn
With urgency and desire—
But I'm stuck instead in this
le-thar-gic, lit-er-ary mire.

A Poem is Like a Pomme de Terre

In its natural glory, undisturbed
Bright white blossoms on dark green vines
Gladden the eye, and yet, its true hidden treasure
Is not revealed until you dig it—exposing
Fat nutritious roots just below the surface.

Brush off the clinging dirt. Behold it eye to eye.
Then tote it to the kitchen with murderous intent—
Skin it, chop it or slice it into strips or bits,
Immerse it whole in boiling water or a hot oven
Until it succumbs and softens to a hungry palate,

Enough to be devoured, unmercifully,
Drenched and dripping with butter or sour crème,
Bits of bacon, chunks of cheddar—
Many ways to make it better—
Enhancements to the barren spud.

Words of the emerging poem may rise up from the page
Like potatoes from the soil, raw and unappealing,
Their inherent value wanting imagination and attention
To transform, enrich, dissect or disembowel them—
Needing to be tortured or enticed into a thing.

A Poem is Like a Pomme de Terre (cont)

Embellish their taste with syntax and vocabulary
Till they are pleasing to the ear and eye, poetic culinary
Rendering the thing pleasing and palatable, tantalizing
And delectable as such other earthly delights
As ribeye steak and fresh green beans.

Not A-mused
       (a Tanka)

the reluctant words
need cajoling to emerge
but my stubborn muse
won't pick up my urgent calls
I hate the obstinate bitch

Per Apps

I read four poems before breakfast today
on my smartphone app, before succumbing
to the call of Facebook posts and notifications,
accumulated texts, messages, and emails,
before I checked the weather forecast.

One poem described
God's disappointment and tough love
banishing clueless Eve and "blameless" Adam
from their home
in the Garden.

The second poem spoke of men
suffering grotesque wounds
earned in battles on foreign lands
far from home and comfort, dying
cursing God.

Meanwhile, the neglected coffee cooled
in my souvenir mug, too tepid to be tempting,
no longer that just-apt temperature
to enhance my insentient bites of apple Danish.

I read the next poem in silence.
It spoke of the sparrows'
ingratitude for gratuitous seed—
and of growing old.

Per Apps (cont)

Another reference to biblical allegory,
titled *Noah's Complaint*,
Spoke of rain—fluttering rain,
fists of rain, acres of rain.

The weather app calls for
more rain today,
possible thunderstorms,
an unseasonal high of 72.

Progress

Black marks on a white page
An irregular array in regular straight lines
Spaces between some marks, not others
Spaces between some lines, not others
Surely sorcery, some demonic witchery

Once carved in stone
Painted on papyrus or rock walls
Artfully crafted on the scraped skin of sheep
Millennia before the Chinese welded fibers with water
Bones and bamboo inscribed with word pictures—hanzi

Hieroglyphics, runes, glyphs, strokes, cursives, fonts
Musings, certainties, uncertainties, truths,
Concepts, legends, lies claimed to be truths,
Spoken lore unnecessary now,
Thoughts ignited in the mind from images called words

Few possessed the sacred knowledge
A thing we now call writing
Recording thoughts with symbols
Preserving thoughts, wisdom, trivia
Transmitting thoughts through space and time

Progress (cont)

Books and bibliotheca
Preserve the knowledge of all humanity—
Law, religion, science, fantasy, pornography
Transmitted through time, independent of time—
Yet, the written word requires a reader

Cursive becomes a secret code
Invisible, impermanent bits and bytes
Share information and misinformation
Instantly across the globe—
Deciphered only by microchip brains

TikTok, Snapchat, Instagram
Render even words redundant
With instantaneous emoticons
Virtual encrypted moving petroglyphs
Embedded within imperfect silicon neurons

Progress?

Ekphrasis on Poetry on a Page
(commentary on visual works of art)

Letters that the words comprise
26 diminutive works of art—
Depending on one's chosen font,
Gothic-like or art nouveau
Some with baroque flourishes
Rendering them almost illegible
Or sturdy, functional Times New Roman
The writer's friend—

The visible atomic structures
Of black words
Arranged on the white sheet
In couplets or rhythmic blocks
Or whimsically haphazard in apparent disarray
Before being lifted from the page
By the poet's voice to fly
And disappear into the reader's mind

Nevermore

Raven or crow
I really don't know,
But its beak should show
Which species it is—

Or the shape of its tail
Or its overall size
Could help me surmise
The truth.

But it would be a surprise
For all fans of Poe
If not raven but crow
Quoth the word Nevermore.

Ghost Writers

What compels the hesitant writer to again take pen to the blank page?
At the core of the myriad reasons why writers write is the insistent need to communicate with some known or unknown fellow inhabitant of the planet Earth, to leave a legacy of words that lay bare one's most inner thoughts, aspirations, contemplations, fears, seek elusive truths, express wisdom, glee or rage, or provoke a hearty belly laugh.
There is solace in words, the reading and the writing of them. The words of poets through the centuries sing of nightingales, the bitter and the sweet of love, or dark death. Writers share their words and all they embody across all time and space. Their gift of words is unwrapped one line upon the next—flowing or tumbling like water in a stream, revealing the poet's soul through the rippled shadows.
My hesitant hand moves now across the page, scant homage to those who have taken up the quill of life before and, like me, wrote.

my remains lie here
among nouns and action verbs
on these white pages

Tattered Pages

Upon the tattered pages
The wisdom of the ages,
Some other's literary creation
Challenging my imagination.

Descriptions of an alien world,
The music of a brook, all this
Has sometimes come to me
On the pages of a book.

Philosophy and ancient creed,
Tales of a place far flung,
And poems I have yet to read
Songs that are unsung,

Recipes for happiness—and pie
A hero's strife in distant lands—
So now, I wish that when I die
I'll hold a book still in my hands.

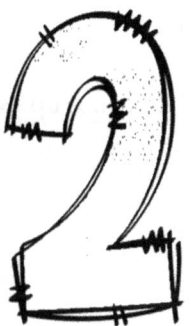

In three words, I can sum up everything I've learned about life: It goes on.

Author unknown

Big Tip

My imagination aroused
When I heard it espoused
That time
Is like money,

As if
Life can be bought
And paid for
With cash or with checks.

If that much is true
Don't seek to accrue
Or watch
For a holiday sale.

If our moments are spent
Like a dollar or cent
Let it rip—
And leave a big tip.

Golden Years

It's your golden years, don't you know,
When giddy-up turns into whoa.
A chance to relax
Before life slips
Right through the cracks.

Let in the good times.
Let out your slacks.
No clock to punch.
Have an early lunch
If that's your desire.

What's one more inch
On that spare tire?
Let the phone ring
Right off the hook
While you just sit back

And enjoy your book
Of poetry or prose.
But just suppose you had a chance
For new adventure, a fresh romance.
Would it really have such strong appeal

Or feel more like a fresh ordeal?
So, put your feet up. Have a drink.
You know it's later than you think.
Don't waste your time on trivia
Like writing down lines

With shaky rhymes—like this.

Playing Games

They gathered around the kitchen table,
The teenage girl and boy
The middle aged woman
And the old gray man,
His daughter and grandchildren.

Their simple satisfying repast of
Pizza with a side of Polish pickles was finished,
The sharing of the day's news complete,
The second glass of red wine poured
To sip and savor leisurely.

Game time, someone said,
And they played mind games
Mixing fact with fiction,
Musings and mirth with affected outrage,
And unsupported opinion

Until the hours spun away
With little attention to their secret thoughts
Of tomorrow's obligations and opportunities,
The mundane necessities of life,
The recognition and contemplation of death.

Playing Games (cont)

They parted, withdrawing into previous preoccupations—
The girl envisioning a bright future,
The boy ruminating video gaming strategies,
The woman to her grocery list and past loves,
The old man simply grateful for another day.

New Year's Eve

Last day.
Final moments.
A conclusion.
A beginning,
Janus peers
Into the fading past
And an arbitrary future—
A fleeting moment
Becomes the nascent present.

We drink
Our quiet cup of kindness,
Toasting auld lang syne.
Reluctantly,
Expectantly,
Hopelessly
We welcome the tomorrows
And their uncertain chances
Yesterday's memories in our hearts.

Love and Learn

We were taught when we were young,
knowing little of love or abstract concepts,
just this: one cannot love an inanimate object—
such things as colored rocks or cold, silent birds.

True enough perhaps, yet wholly insufficient,
Not nailing the true essence of love, i.e.
Love is not an abstraction,
As necessary as air, love sustains the living.

Joy and sorrow, love and grief inseparable
True love is durable, indestructible, eternal,
unyielding to space or time even beyond death's door
unto tomorrow and tomorrow and tomorrow.

Kintsukuroi
(Japanese pottery-repair art celebrating transience
        and *imperfection*)

The glass shade of our bedside lamp,
  decorated with a spray of pale rose blossoms,
is further imbued with an array of *jagged* glue lines,
      fragile *fragments* reattached,
the *imperfect* shining globe
              made more than whole.

Far from detracting from its beauty,
     the *lines* enhance,
        convey a message:
Broken can be repaired,
         though not restored,
yet restoring comfort and light to our *imperfect* lives.

Kintsukuroi (cont)

A patina of *use* and *abuse* decorates
  much of what we own and love and who we are—
covert lines of surgeries mending *broken* bones and bodies.
And what maze of random *cracks*, failures and *fissures*
might confront our eyes if our *souls* were on display?

Flaws and *imperfections* that make us whole and *human*,
              lines of *disrepair*
      on *spirits* not recovered from lost loves, lost lives,
          concealed *trauma* lines
failing to restore a still-broken heart.

Yet, are we not altogether more worthy,
        stronger, of greater purpose, relevance and beauty
  than our pristine undamaged bodies, minds and souls
by our *testing*, our *aging*, our *mending*,
        our survival?

Changing Dimensions

Just an awkward scratch at first
That uncertain line in first grade or kindergarten,
Then two up and one across make an H.
Later, we learn it is the shortest distance
Between two points—
Unless you make is it less stern, more graceful
With curves in one or more directions
Like S or a yellow smiley face.

Then Euclid shows how lines make geometric spaces,
And x and y coordinates map out a graph in
Two dimensions to define a supple curve
With simple numbers—
Even the rigid straight line needs
Two components, mathematical yin and yang
To orient it in flat earth space.

Adding height to length and breadth
We finally acknowledge the third dimension
We knew was lurking there all the while.
Reality, but not so easily represented
On a flat scrap of paper
As by merely glancing
Up and down and around the room.

My gaze settles on the colonial chairs
With high H-shaped backs, her favorites,
Or on the lift-chair where she spent her last days
On this heavenly blue sphere
Or on the 12 by 16 rectangle on the wall
That does not answer when I speak to her.

Changing Dimensions (cont)

But mathematicians tell us we need at least one more
Dimension to describe our expanding universe
And many more are available if we need them.
An infinite number really, why stop with two or three
Or four
Yet when you shrink that line, that scratch, that
    Shortest distance
Between two points,
It becomes a mere dot, a point with no dimension
That quietly fades away.

One Day

Walking hand-in-hand
along the summer shore of a great lake
they came upon drifted wood
washed up from some other place
polished smooth and clean of bark.

"Take this one,"
she said of a certain piece of hardwood limb,
gracefully curved from the heavy end
where it had once attached to where it ended,
broken and jagged like craggy mountain peaks.
"Maybe you can make a lamp of it."

He can remember the long labor of evening the base
so it would stand, straight, firm and balanced,
cleaning sand from worn crevices and cracks, and
affixing a socket with a switch at the top—but
especially the making of the foot-long hole
to carry the electrical cord from base to pinnacle.

"It's perfect," she said at last
and found a shade to complete the transformation
from nature's discard to a thing of grace and utility
that stood on a table in their living room for years.

With fading memory, he wonders now,
Whatever became of our driftwood lamp?

Seasoned

She preferred ranch dressing;
He really liked blue cheese.
She complained of differences,
"It seems he always disagrees."

He wondered and he pondered
What can I ever do to please,
To quench the fires of her desires
Before love between us flees?

Until at last they both despaired,
The twain was never met.
They went their very separate ways
Full of rancor and regret.

Each alone, while years rolled by
Until they met again one day
With shattered, shuttered feelings
Wondering, *How could it end that way?*

With wrinkled hands and hopeful hearts
They remembered days when love first called
When they first found each other's arms
Before she lost her figure, and he was going bald.

So now again the two are one—
They sing life's sweetest ballad
And share an aged, mellowed love
And vinaigrette on their salad.

The Thought
Prompted by the poem The Lost Chord
by Adelaide Anne Porter (1825-1864)

(one excerpted stanza)
I have sought, but I seek it vainly,
That one lost chord divine
Which came from the soul of the organ,
And entered into mine.

The Thought

came to me unbidden
full of wisdom and of charm
and I thought to keep it ever
secure from change or harm

when the needs and obligations
of yet another task-filled day
burst upon my restless mind
and the thought refused to stay.

Now I've searched my mind for hours
wanting—needing to recall
that sweet but now forgotten thought
that seemed to say it all.

The Thought (cont)

Will that banished, vanished thought
on some furtive, fleeting day return
to calm my troubled mind
and settle in at last to stay—

perhaps to be recalled at will
while all other thoughts have failed
to comfort and assure my soul
when the joys of life have paled.

cave man

what i remember most about the ice age
besides the persistent hunger
and my first taste of fire-meat
is that it was damned cold
i mean
the eternal bone chilling chill
even given the thick furry skins
used to wrap my own thick hide
like that of all my neanderthal brothers and sisters

of course we did not call ourselves that
a name applied to our ancestral remains
discovered in the shelter of my cave home
many millennia later

we were just folks
trying to make a living in a world with
only primitive tools and communications
where the average temperature was cold enough
to keep mammoth meat fresh from moon to moon

but who among us would have conceived
of what the stars or we are made of
or bosons or viruses or super walmarts
before we perished one by one
and disappeared
but for our bones
from this place
you call
planet
earth

The Final Mystery

We laugh at flat earth folks,
sneer, disparage, denigrate,
armed with superior science
our absorbent minds assimilated
in third grade
without question.

But which of us
has wit enough
to first imagine

our whirling blue globe
floating in darkness
yet tethered
to the sun and fellow travelers
by unseen bonds
of a thing we call gravity
in an ever expanding universe—
distant galaxies,
bright stars, unseen black holes,
matter and antimatter,
somethings,
and
less than nothings,

much less explain
why are we here?

Ode and haiku for Covid-19

The trees still know it's spring.
The birds still sing at dawn—
    then, unaware, take wing
    while our humanity has gone,
    and the bells no longer ring
in yesterday's Babylon.

at the Walmart store
a furtive glance averted
above the face mask

Miasma on America

Stealthy stench of fear,
distrust, ignorance and hate,
substituting
lies for facts,
might for right,
accusation for consideration—

pernicious emanation
more deadly than
the aerosol of viral contagion
that infects our precious air,
not preventable by masks,
exacerbated by distancing,

but curable
by inoculations
of fairness, fact,
understanding of the truth—
immunization by
respect and love.

We are one people,
one nation . . .
Indivisible?

We Need a Change of Climate

It should come as no surprise
That we watch oceans rise,
Yet still there are folks
Who insist it's a hoax
By some devilish scientists
Lurking about in our midst.

Floods and great storms,
A twenty year drought—
Don't worry—just pray
Surely that'll bail us out,
Just act cavalier—
Have some pizza and beer.

We've landed robots on Mars
Yet shun electrical cars.
Did God give us a brain
And a thing call free will?
To discover God's plan
Is the scientist's thrill.

Can we humans survive
The immeasurable cost?
Better turn on those brains
Before all is lost.
We're today's dinosaurs
If Ignorance scores.

Apocalypse Revised

The book of poems lies abandoned beside the open window as season passes into season, year passes into year and century into century.

Daffodils bloom outside each spring, and acorns fall from the tall oak tree onto the fertile soil each autumn before winter snows cover the earth.

Each summer, creeper vines ascend higher, reaching, grasping the brick wall with tenuous tendrils, content at last to rest beneath the eaves.

Gentle breezes turn the brittle pages of the ancient book. Sunlight touches the fading words, turns the aging paper brown and fragile.

A small gray bird flutters down and struts upon the open window sill, curious to see the pages turning by an unseen hand.

Satisfied, it cocks its head and flicks its tail and flies onto the branches of the tall oak tree to sing its cheerful four-note melody.

No hand remains to close the cover of the weathered book or shutter the window.

No human eye beholds the faded words that cover the pages with uncertain patterns.

No sapient mind now labors to understand the thoughts inscribed upon the pages.

No human heart thrills to the images the poet once had captured and offered to humanity.

better
ember
than
ash

There is pleasure in the pathless woods,
There is rapture on the lonely shore,
There is society, where none intrudes,
By the deep sea, and music in its roar:
I love not man the less, but Nature more

Lord Byron

spring green leaves
dancing wildly on the branches
then the rain

yellow bird
in the rain
singing

tiny goldfinch
deathly still in my hand
still warm

after the rain
the robin cocks his head
the worm's journey ends

disgruntled robin
probing springtime morning frost
comes up empty

camera captures
green iridescent feathers
blurred wings beat free

tiny winged warrior
guardian of the nectar
before the journey

springtime breezes
do you smell
the lilacs too?

dog days of summer
heat and drought and thunderstorms
are you Sirius?

autumn leaves
are your memories
colorful too?

winter blankets
none so warm as
last night's snow

fly on my plate
didn't ask me
to share

fly on the wall
daring me
to swat

pesky,

    devil fly

nothing   better to
                               do

                 devil

than be

         me

black ant
        exploring the porcelain sink
                are you brave or lost?

snowflake

are you sure

you're different

humble dandelion
bright yellow royalty
in early spring

one tenacious leaf
flutters in the autumn breeze
another day takes flight

pewter autumn skies
barren branches cold and gray
one last yellow rose

through the morning mist
bright scarlet leaves float to earth
a bird song rises

puffed up cardinal
wears audacious camouflage
I see him sleeping

silver frost crystals
shining in the morning sun
liquefy and die

rays of golden dawn
streak the frigid autumn sky
casting cold shadows

full moon rising
shifting shadows
weaving memories

       moonlit shadows
  in the long and silent night
she snuggles closer

Honest good humor is the oil and wine of a merry meeting, and there is no jovial companionship equal to that where the jokes are rather small and the laughter abundant.

Washington Irving

Humor is something that thrives between man's aspirations and his limitations. There is more logic in humor than in anything else because, you see, humor is truth.

Victor Borge

Charlotte the Harlot

Had a heart of solid gold.
Sold her body, not her soul,
Knew all the sundry ways to please
A subtle sigh, a certain squeeze.
Knew all the tricks and even more,
Enticed men by the clothes she wore.
Shy first timers, corporate elite—
Once they came, they'd all repeat
Their visits to her welcome thighs.

Then she died—what a sad surprise!
But no one claimed her or inquired
When so sadly she expired.
So her clients gathered to confer
What in the name of heaven or hell
Should, at last, they do with her,
Burial or quick cremation?

They dug deep for a donation
For a lovely red-lined casket,
A funeral and flowers by the basket—
And to pay the undertaker extra,
When she at last was laid to rest,
To fulfill her very last bequest
And arrange her for eternity
In the position she loved best.

Spring Ahead

I saved some time this morning—
One hour to be exact.
Or was it just taken from me
By some government contract
I didn't approve or ever sign,
Yet I'm required to comply.

I'm up early now—almost awake
And the sun's up in the sky.
Perhaps the hour is just a loan
Held in some celestial vault
Until in fall we pay it off
And fall back like we ought.

All these annual temporal swings
Can be really quite confusing,
But I know these things for sure:
Right now, I'd rather be a-snoozing.
And saving time can soon lose interest—
Resetting 15 clocks is not at all amusing.

Thanks for Nothing, Robert Pinsky

Pinsky advised, "Write a poem about a word,"
and I chose plenitude
for little better reason than I thought
I knew its meaning and was pleased (amused, delighted)
by the sound of its name, its feeling in my mouth.
I looked it up on Webster's online dictionary to be sure
and found two definitions listed, 1. and 2..

The first was completeness; the second abundancy,
giving me some pause, because
while I was familiar with the second,
the first held subtle differences in its definition, and
the two seemed not totally congruent
(for if they were, there would be no need for both).

Though both convey a sense of comfort
to the mind with
soothing satisfaction,
the first might be so much more
or perhaps so much less than the second,
depending on one's wants and needs.

Then came a plenitude of synonyms
(itself a rarity in possession of two Ys)
55 to be exact, as well as 32 antonyms
being in some fashion opposed.
Yet each new word held nuances of its own
and possibly as many likes and un-likes.

Thanks for Nothing, Robert Pinsky (cont)

How can I swim through the undercurrents of fistful
carload, gobs, passel, potful, profusion, scads and wads
for example, to make my own singular choice
with its own internal conflicts, much less deal with
pittance, smidgen, speck or trace, which
are meant to amplify by showing opposition?

This abundancy of information
neither sated nor fulfilled
with a completeness of new knowledge,
but left me perplexed by Pinsky's proposition
bemused, still seeking satisfaction
from a poem about plenitude.

Parting Impression

There once was a gangster named Knute
Who robbed a bank in his birthday suit.
Said the teller named Grace,
I can't remember his face,
But his butt was really quite cute.

Heavenly Advice

If by faith, by good works or by guile
You avoid heaven's circular file
Even though you are late
Rush right in through that gate
And be sure to give Peter a smile

He Who Hesitates . . .

Don't delay when it's your time to go
Don't say "Well, I really don't know!"
If those gates open wide,
You'd better scurry inside,
Or you might end up way down below.

A Matter of Some Gravity

I have run a marathon
(god, I thought I'd die)
and swam a mile shore to shore,
but no matter how I try
there's no way that I can fly.

I can hit a golf ball
(I once had a par).
I can throw a football
(though not very far).
I can fry an egg.
I can bake a pie.
I can jump at least three feet,
but I cannot fly.

I can write a poem,
and I have written prose.
I can grow tomatoes,
and I can prune a rose.
I can play guitar
And sing sweet melodies
(though I prefer the classics
recorded on CDs).

A Matter of Some Gravity (cont)

I have fought a bully—
punched him in the eye!
I succeed at many things,
but no matter
how I try,
struggling
with all my might,
I simp-ly . . . can-not   fly.

Birds do it.
Bees do it.
Even butterflies do it.
So tell me, if you think you can:
Why, oh why, can't I
fly?

To Err

I have flaws
Because
I am human,
Whereas (forgive me),

Were I divine,
My flaws
Would exist
Without cause

Despair the Hare

The children cried
The adults sighed
But still they tried
To have a happy Easter

'cause the Bunny landed
Empty handed
And just sat there
On his keester

No eggs to hide
Far and wide
No yummy
Chocolate bunny

No marshmallow treat
They loved to eat
Not a single jelly bean
For which they were so keen

Empty baskets, without hope
No thoughts on how to cope
That year the Easter Bunny
Was a great big Easter Dope.

Dating Protocol

On more than one occasion
A kind of dating agitation
Resulted from what he thought to be
Politeness and consideration.

Reluctant to demand or to direct,
He'd give her the option to select
What movie they might go to view
Or which of several things they'd do.

But she'd defer from doing that,
"Don't leave the choices up to me,
Just pick a number from your hat."
So he offered her more options—two or three

Alternatives to consider and explore
Until, at length, she finally chose
Her own, out-of-nowhere, dark-horse,
Number Four.

What Ever Happened to Eclectic

He'd never heard the word before
the year he turned age thirty-five
when it burst upon the linguistic scene
like a delinquent teenager late for dinner.
He consulted Webster's Dictionary
to understand its meaning:

*An approach that synthesizes the best
elements from a variety of sources,
or one who employs such an approach.*
He considered the concept fit
his own philosophy
of learning rather well.

Others also felt attracted to the term,
which henceforth soon appeared
wherever he looked—or didn't—
magazine articles, advertisements,
even the name of a Rock and Roll band—
until it seemed impossible to avoid.

But having lost its sheen at last
from when he first encountered it,
it withdrew into vernacular oblivion
as suddenly as it had appeared
as popular jargon almost always does
while he still

synthesizes away.

Autumnal

There's a nip in the air,
I don't care.
It's autumn.

Colored leaves
On the trees,
It must be autumn.

Long sleeve shirts
Replace the tees,
When it's autumn.

Temps tempting freezing,
Ragweed spores have people sneezing.
A-choo, it's autumn.

Wind back the clock, shed a tear,
Cold weather's near,
But it's still autumn.

Skies blue and clear
Winter's almost here—
Last days of autumn.

Now pumpkin-spice
Tastes really nice in a Starbucks cup,
Now you know it's really fall, y'all.

Unspoiled

Their eyes met across the bar.
She said, "My place isn't very far."
So he took her home on just a whim.
(She looked better when the lights were dim.)

He said, "Maybe we should have a chat,"
And they talked at length of this and that,
Until he saw it was half past three
And departed with his chastity.

5

You call it madness, but I call it love.

Song lyric by Russ Columbo, Con Conrad, Gladys DuBois, and Paul Gregory. 1931

The Road We Took

I liked to wander off the beaten path
Never admitting to being lost.
She felt secure with the safety of a map
And begged me to ask strangers for direction.

My world was filled with facts, numbers
    and ambition;
Her world was filled with dreams
    and memories and devotion.
I tended the dry mundane of taxes and budgets;
She decorated for each holiday and in between.

I thrilled to Coltrane and Beethoven;
She loved Neal Diamond and marching bands.
I mowed the lawn and gassed and oiled the cars;
She sent the children off to school
    in clean, pressed clothes
As good as new from the Goodwill store.

I read Scientific American and studied
Constellations in the cold night air;
She read In Touch and Us and watched
Dancing With the Stars on television.

I studied ancient forms of poetry;
She informed me of the latest news.
I planned for a far distant retirement, an empty nest;
She planned for joyous weekend outings with the kids.

I loved her
Through all our glory years, and strife;
I know she loved me too—
And that made all the difference.

Ice cream and Cookies

Maybe what I loved most
Was the little girl in her—
How she thrilled to the marching bands
Playing Sousa on Independence Day.

Her ooh and aahs for fireworks after dark,
Her delight with plastic participation floating,
Falling gently to rest upon the varied scenes
In snow globes she collected.

Her love of animals,
From the fiercest jungle creature
To the puppy cuddled in her lap,
And cardinals in the persimmon tree.

And ice cream and cookies—
Always ice cream and cookies.

in the deep of night
her hand brushes my shoulder
tornado sirens

Tremors

A small misstep, a stumble, just a silly wobble.
Her hand shakes, almost imperceptibly, penning
    a brief note to a loved one.
Still legible, though diminished, vanishing later
    into indecipherable scribbles.

"What day is it?"
Yet, "Oh, yes. You had better buy some birthday cards."

Some effects of Parkinson's Disease are well known.
The tremors that splatter soup from a tremulous spoon.
The shuffle that eventually makes even a few steps
    a valiant, arduous effort.
Okay, we can live with even that.

Advanced effects may be more profound. More deadly.
Creeping loss of muscle and motor control.
Stealthy dementia, slowly fogging the brightest mind.

Speaking, chewing, swallowing—a studied effort, until .
.
bedtime ritual
her bright blue eyes seeking mine
lips move, I yuv you

Perhaps, the phantoms will not visit her tonight.

Pas de Deux
(a dance duet)

She loved to dance.
Considered it for a vocation once.
Or might have been a fly-girl,
but her mother wouldn't sign.

She attended Teacher's College instead.
More practical. We met there and dated.
She taught me how to dance.
The waltz, the polka, others, always counting out the
rhythm to guide my steps.

She had many other beaus, but she waited
while I wasn't ready, while I served my military duty,
until I finally proposed on one knee
offering the solitary diamond I'd purchased in
Amsterdam.

She said yes. We danced at our wedding
before our weekend honeymoon in the Windy City.
She counted and I moved my feet.
One two three. Open, open, close.

Now we dance a ritual dance
without the sound of music.
I hold her close to lift her from the wheelchair
into her cushioned La-Z-Boy.

Pas de Deux (cont)

She settles back.
I raise her lifeless legs.
I punch the TV remote
to find *Dancing With the Stars*.

She smiles as if saying thank you,
but I wonder, in her silent world,
does she still count for me
as we dance our quiet pas de deux?

One Day at a Time

Oh, how she loved music.
Neil Diamond, Kenny Rogers, Humperdinck,
The Oakridge Boys—a select few of favorites,
Songs of an earlier era,
songs from her childhood and young womanhood.
Songs from our dating days, *Because of You*—
a must request at every dance—a favorite of mine too.

My preferences ran more to jazz and the classics
Beethoven, Puccini, Ella, Brubeck, Coltrane.
We met somewhere in the middle with the wonders of
Rogers and Hammerstein and Andrew Lloyd Webber,
until one day twenty years ago, a tumor
stole her hearing, and the music died.

Oh, she loved to dance.
Might have made it a career
before settling on the more practical work of
teaching first-graders to sing and dance and read,
and the less glamorous life of a wife and mother.

She taught me too—
The waltz, the two-step, the polka (our specialty),
others, though I preferred the slow romantics
her close and sweet in my arms
moving gentle to the music.

One Day at a Time (cont)

And then, not one day, but gradually
she could no longer walk or dance.

Simple pleasures, critical abilities
abandoned her.
Disabilities attacked her
one day at a time
almost imperceptibly at first
then with increased vigor and cruelty
claimed her independence.

She with scarce complaint,
while even her speech and bright smile,
in inexorable time, became labors of love.

And then one day
she died.

The Garden

It was a weeping cherry. She called it her fairy tree—
drooping branches loaded with abundant blossoms
pink and white each springtime.

Then it withered one year, without cause it seemed,
and died.
And she died too, before the warmth of spring.

Removing the roots was the hardest part,
so I could spade up the earth where the tree had grown
to plant a garden that she would never view.

Flowering shrubs—a spectrum of color—now bask in
the sun where the cherry tree had once cast its shadows,
but I wonder if she would approve.

What I Mean

When I say *I miss her* . . .
It is not just the admissions
Of love at bedtime that I speak,
It is the memory of meeting, unaware
Of what the next 70 years would bring—
The awesome gift of love
The steadfast commitment
The terrible anguish of parting.

When I say *I miss her*
I mean her broad or subtle
Or cunning or come-hither smiles.
I mean the shape of her breasts and
The touch of her body gentle against me
In the dark.

I mean the shared joys and trials
Of rearing four children. The special family
Holiday rituals she planned and managed every year
And that brought such happiness and memories to us all.
I mean
How brilliantly she spoke at times
Of matters I never knew
And never knew she knew,
The many arts and crafts created
With clever mind and careful hand.

What I Mean (cont)

When I say *I miss her*
I mean the laughs we have laughed
And the tears we have shed together
Holding fast, together, tight.
I mean waking her at morning light
Her bright blue eyes revealed.
I mean hearing
Hi, how was your day?
Or *Are you sure you're alright*
When she knew, of course, I wasn't.

I mean the faint scent of Chanel
From the small bottle of Number 5
I bought for her years and years ago
Reserved for only special occasions.

When I say *I miss her*
I mean her quiet, constant support
In my own darkest, desperate hours.
I mean especially her bright laugh
So sadly sequestered near the end.
I mean her gutsy, gritty, forthright self
I so admired even the very first time
I saw her. Until the very last.

What I Mean (cont)

I mean the myriad memories
That strike at random night and day—
All this in every bright flash
Untold times each day.
All this and so much more.

After so many years
Two divided by anything
Is not one.

Sometimes

I wondered
If she really knew
How much I loved her

Until she died
And then

I wondered
If I ever knew
How much I loved her

This above all: to thine own self be true, and it must follow, as the night the day, thou canst not then be false to any man.

W. Shakespeare

Auto Biography

Born in the year
Nineteen hundred thirty two

Saw a bit of our green planet
Sailed upon the ocean blue

Made so many mistakes, but
Found my love, long and true

Learned chemistry, physics, advanced math
But learned that 1 plus 1 can be greater than 2

I've watched the midnight sun
Walked barefoot in the morning dew

Ran a marathon—
Just thought it was the thing to do

Made many plans,
Did a few

Good lord the time,
How it flew

Until just now, the end of the year
Twenty hundred and twenty two

Optimist

By the age of ninety
New firsts are rare
Though one doesn't really care
For excitement and adventure as much
As another day of peace and quiet,
A good BM, a healthy diet.

And while most firsts are in the past
One knows not which will be the last—
To stand up straight and breathe sweet air
Rewards as much as a hot affair
Once did in youthful days of yore,
I say as much, yes even more.

Change and daring are not the rage
They once were at that distant age.
Give me the Now and Constancy—
I'll never climb another tree.
And yet, I'm not a weeping mourner
Fearful of what's just around the corner.

I welcome each new day I'm dealt
Grateful for all the things I've felt
In living all these many years
The agony, the ecstasy
The joyful smiles
The woeful tears.

Optimist (cont)

I'd be happy for a few years more.
(Life has never, ever been a bore.)
To seek out new knowledge, even friends,
The thrill of being never ends,
So, I'll be looking for the next new twist,
Now that I'm a nonagenarian optimist.

Change of Pace

I used to walk when I was young
Welcoming the gentle rain.
But soon I scurried through the drops,
Ah, but to be young again.

When I was even younger still
I'd never walk. I always ran
Down city street, up country hill.
Oh, to be young again.

The years sped by, and I slowed down.
Still, I entered races as a man
With burning lungs and aching limbs.
If only I were young again.

The urge to run no longer calls
Now I just hobble, best I can,
Lucky still to walk this earth,
Ah, but to be young again.

The Meaning of Life—at Last

A century after the quantum revolution,
the nature of reality is still a mystery.
Tom Siegfried, Science News, 15 January 2022

I have always questioned.
Authority. Alleged facts. Assertions of philosophers and priests.
A real doubting Thomas—that just seems unlikely as hell.

I debated our local preacher on religion when I was twelve.
He resorted to prayer for his rebuttal. Not a fair fight.
I remained dissatisfied still seeking understanding.

Eden or Evolution? The universe? Time?
The chemistry and physics of all things—
What is the miracle of Life?

Metaphysics.
The yin and the yang.
What is the meaning of life?

A lifetime to contemplate endless questions.
Now I am happy to report—
It all remains a mystery.

I am

(I)

I am here
I am now
I am all my yesterdays

I am many, not one
Each perceived in the eye
Of a different beholder

I am scientist
And philosopher
And gazer of stars

I am father, grandfather, great grandfather
Grateful to be so blessed
And yet, I am alone

I am old
I am tired
And yet, I am

(II)

I am a poet
And a writer of prose
When you read what I write
Please don't hold your nose

Parental Guidance

Dad taught me

How to hurl a baseball, fast and true,
Plant and prune tomato plants,
Which was bolt and which was screw,

To crack and fry an egg in grease
And cook the bacon flat,
When to begin and when to cease.

To pause a bit and say the grace
Before Mom's delicious meal.
To shave the whiskers from my face,

To shine my shoes, to tie my ties
To shake a hand with a grip that's firm
And look into the other man's eyes,

To drive an ancient Buick
With four gears on the floor,
Change a tire . . . all that and more.

Mom taught me

That honesty is the greatest virtue,
And
How to say son-of-a-bitch in German.

Late Awakening

Clanking of the furnace grate sent sounds of clashing armor to our sleeping ears. We huddled near floor registers where the first indistinct wafts of warmed air rose from the basement furnace to our cold, dark second-story flat.
Below, Dad stoked and coaxed feeble, dying embers into renewed life and built the coal fire on the furnace grate to heat another Wisconsin winter day.
Warm light shone into the cheerless bedroom hallway from the kitchen where Mom waited at the table with two cups of fresh, black steaming coffee and four empty bowls.
A pot of thick Quaker Oatmeal or Cream of Wheat waited on the stovetop while bleary eyed children dressed and shuffled toward the welcome light, accepting without question.

gratuitous love
unquestioned and ungrateful
cherished memories

Q and A

I did not view my parents as other people until I became one myself. A parent that is, not a people.

Prior to that, my parents were on a plane above myself, above others. Trusted sources of the truth, never to be doubted. Some lessons sought after, some imposed. How to tie your shoes or dry your butt after a shower. When, why and how to say, "How do you do?' and offer a sturdy handshake. Practical matters.

Not at all obvious or trivial things. Simple and complex questions of childhood and youth. How many pennies in a dollar? Why do religions that proffer love hate each other? How did life begin? What is the soul made of?

But never, How do you feel? How did you fall in love? What makes you tremble in the night? Until the parent-child bond transformed, matured. Until it was too late.

> *now, long since*
> *grand children ask*
> *are we there yet*

Once

I knew a girl with yellow hair
bright as the morning sun
in the warm summer sky.
It fell soft upon her shoulders
and wafted easy in the evening breeze.

Her eyes, of uncertain hue,
like wildflowers in early spring,
undemanding but intolerant
of all except the truth,
welcomed or banished in a blink.

Her startlingly soft lips
provoked
both caution and passion
when we first kissed
and later

when she whispered
in my unsuspecting ear, carefully,
like a child's confession—I love you.
Now, in my long winter,
I wonder why we parted then.

Saved

On the silver screen, the hero
places a slim book of poems in his left breast pocket
or a fine print pocket bible, the pages worn, or a packet
of letters declaring undying love, tied with yellow
ribbon
or a shiny silver cigarette case, a gift from his beloved.

He is saved from death as he faces an unseen enemy—
death from a well-placed shot he never heard.
He returns to the arms of his true love,
her gift severely damaged but intact,
to live a full and happy life together.

None of my books
of poems are pocket size.
I own no bible, diminutive or large
nor could I read the fine print now, even if I did.
I did own a cigarette case once—was it a gift from her?

I gave up smoking, advice from the Surgeon General.
My breast pocket is empty except for an occasional note
to remind me to buy radishes or eggs or Kleenex tissue;
I've saved the letters she wrote when our love was new.
They save me every time.

Sanctum

We knew each other then—
Discovered bit by bit, each
Inner nook and cranny, each
Sensitivity and unspoken desire,
Pleasure and displeasure.

And still
Some hidden mysteries
Would never see the light
Of each other's day—
Mysteries of formation, transformation.

Loves and hates and
How stone walls were built
Around her heart
Where I might find a secret stile
One day— or she might reach across.

Though she did not
Belong to me
I could not bear
She might belong
To any other.

Sanctum (cont)

I persevered.
She came to me
Still holding some intrigues
Intact in some sheltered place
That made me love her more.

Vulnerable

She allowed me to enter her
life, and I didn't
use protection

My Way

No need to know east from west,
north from south, or the way home from anywhere
when Mom or Dad held tight my hand
to guide me there.

Guidance could be relied upon from
uncles and aunts, preachers and teachers
and the streetcar conductor,
ready to act as my ad hoc instructor.

Bosses and sergeants came a bit later in life,
marching along to the drum and the fife
marking the rhythm and showing the way
no need for me to have something to say.

Finally I searched out my own new directions,
made hard decisions while going astray,
living and learning with close introspection
stumbling along life's meandering way.

Detours and crossroads oft' loomed ahead
detracting, delaying the progress I sought
persisting, pursuing with hope and not dread
building a life on the way, as I'd ought.

.

My Way (cont)

When other hands reached out for my own
seeking the lessons I'd learned in my day
I prayed and I strove
to not lead them astray

Looking back now, now that most is the past,
nothing can change, even I would,
but what have I left that ever may last,
except that I did the best that I could.

From morning star to sunset's blaze
passing hours, fleeting days, no time now
to regret or atone, still searching for
that singular way—my own way home.

Again

When I was only twenty-three
I never thought that I would see
What little now is left of me

When I turned a robust forty-five
Doing all the right things to survive
It felt great to be alive

The sands were sifted through the glass
Scant notice how the years had passed
Untold regrets and joys amassed

Then suddenly the years were spent
Can't comprehend how fast they went
Few days left to reflect, repent

Now, with those few hours that remain
With withered body and slowing brain
I'd like to do it all—again

Decrepit

Is a funny word.
I used to like to say it,
But now it's really what I am,
I just could not delay it.

Old and wrinkled, tired and wan,
Can't stand quite erect,
Not very long until I'm gone,
And it won't be on a jet.

Still life goes on
And I go with it
To welcome
Each bright new day

Even though
I'm so,
Very so
Decrepit.

So much fabric. So little time.

a quilter

The Long and the Short of It

Selecting which of the poems I have generated over the past three to four years that now appear in this volume required a good deal of tough love to cast out the orphans and a bit of rationale to retain the chosen. First, six generally related themes seemed to emerge: writing, life, nature, humor, Dolly, and modestly last, my favorite subject—me.

Inspiration for the poems: arose out of dreams, recollections of the near and distant past, or merely watching the world from my kitchen window.

Most of the poems can be considered free verse, i.e. free from standard form whether or not featuring meter or rhyme. A few form poems are included, e.g. Limericks and haibun (a composite of prose with haiku). There is an entire section relating to nature where haiku seems appropriate, in keeping with the ancient, traditional form. This brief poem is deceptively simple. The image or emotion of a moment offered by the poet is meant to evoke a response from the reader, leaving the poet's interpretation unstated. Pause to recognize and express your feelings on each little poem.

Several of the poems in Section 5 were previously published in my memoir, *for the Good Times, a love story*, Vabella Publishing, 2021. These are the poems *Sometimes, Tremors, What I Mean, One Day at a Time, Pas de deux,* and *in the deep of night*.

Limiting the collection to just 90 poems was done arbitrarily to coincide with the number of years I have crawled, walked, run, shuffled and sat on the planet earth, thus 90 years — 90 poems. Could my next collection contain 100?

Acknowledgements

The poets known as the Carrollton Writers Guild have helped tweak, twist, or toss my poetry for many years while we gather to meet at the Carrollton Center for the Arts once each month. Of this group of friends and artists, Eleanor Hoomes and Marc LaFountain critiqued this collection in detail, providing improvements in both quality and quantity. As with my previous poetry and prose works, John Bell of Vabella Publishing provided essential help in bringing this book to press.

www.ingramcontent.com/pod-product-compliance
Lightning Source LLC
Chambersburg PA
CBHW070449050426
42451CB00015B/3404